TEXAS

in words and pictures

BY DENNIS B. FRADIN

MAPS BY LEN W. MEENTS

Consultant:
Claire Williams
Director of Research
Texas Historical Commission

22211

CHILDRENS PRESS ™

CHICAGO

For the Klingelhoffers—Jill, Bill,
Sarah, and Louis

For their help, the author thanks:
   Claire Williams, Texas Historical Commission
   Dr. E. Mott Davis, Professor of Anthropology, University of Texas at A
   Susan Bains, Oil and Gas Librarian, Railroad Commission of Texas
   Virginia Hall, Librarian, Texas Department of Agriculture

Big Bend National Park

Library of Congress Cataloging in Publication Data

Fradin, Dennis B
   Texas in words and pictures.

   SUMMARY: A brief introduction to the land,
history, cities, industries, and famous sites
of the Lone Star State.
   1. Texas—Juvenile literature.   [1. Texas]
I. Meents, Len W.   III.   Title.
F386.3.F7   976.4   80-27497
ISBN 0-516-03943-1

Picture Acknowledgments:
TEXAS STATE DEPARTMENT OF HIGHWAYS AND PUBLIC
TRANSPORTATION—2, 5, 9, 13, 15, 16, 17, 19, 21, 23 (top, below left,
below right), 25 (right), 26 (right), 30, 31 (left), 32, 37, 40
SAN JACINTO MEMORIAL MONUMENT AND MUSEUM—9
TOM WINTER—11, 29, 31 (above)
BEAUMONT CONVENTION AND VISITORS BUREAU—18
NASA—20
TEXAS TOURIST DEVELOPMENT AGENCY—23
DALLAS CHAMBER OF COMMERCE, Convention and Visitors Bureau
24, 25 (left), 26 (left)
FORT WORTH CHAMBER OF COMMERCE—27
JAMES R. LACOMBE, Houston Chamber of Commerce—35
GALVESTON CHAMBER OF COMMERCE—35
CORPUS CHRISTI CONVENTION AND VISITORS BUREAU—36
LYNDON BAINES JOHNSON LIBRARY AND MUSEUM—42
JAMES P. ROWAN—Cover, 44

COVER—Yucca plant in Palo Duro State Park

Texas

The word Texas (TEX • iss) comes from the Caddo Indian word *Tejas,* meaning *friends.* Texas is in the south-central United States. Except for Alaska, Texas is the biggest of our 50 states.

Texas is a leading state in many ways. It is our top state for producing oil. It is the number one state for raising beef cattle and for growing cotton.

Do you know where President Lyndon B. Johnson was born? Or President Dwight D. Eisenhower (EYE • zen • how • er)? Do you know where a famous battle was fought at a place called the Alamo (AL • ah • moh)? Or where scientists control space ships that are 250,000 miles from Earth?

You'll soon see that the answer to all these questions is: Texas, the Lone Star State!

Long before there were people in Texas, dinosaurs ruled the land. Tyrannosaurus Rex (ty • RAN • ah • SORE • us REX) was there. He ate other dinosaurs. Camels roamed about. Sharks swam in areas that are now dry land. Fossils of these ancient animals have been found in Texas.

People first came to Texas over 11,000 years ago. The first Texans were hunters. Their stone spear points have been found. Remains of their camp fires have been found, too.

Thousands of years later, many Indian tribes lived in Texas. The Karankawa (kah • RANK • ah • wah), Coahuiltecan (koh • ah • WEEL • te • can), Tonkawa (TONK • ah • wah), and Lipan Apache (ah • PATCH • ee) were four of the tribes there. The Caddo (CAD • oh) were a group of Indian tribes in east Texas.

Many Texas Indians hunted buffalo with bows and arrows. They ate the meat. They made the skins into clothing. Texas Indians also killed deer and bears. Indians who hunted often lived in tents called *tepees*.

The Caddo Indians hunted, but they also farmed. Corn, beans, and squash were their main crops. Farming meant that the Caddo could settle in one place. They built houses out of logs and grass. A number of such houses formed a village.

Indian drawings at Huaco State Park

The Spanish were the first non-Indians in Texas. In 1519 the Spaniard Alonso Alvarez de Piñeda (al • LON • zo AL • vah • rez day pin • YAY • dah) sailed along the coast of the Gulf of Mexico. He made maps. Piñeda was greeted by friendly Indians.

By the 1530s Spain ruled Mexico (MEX • ih • koh), which is south of Texas. A Spaniard named Coronado (kor • oh • NAH • doh) heard stories about "cities of gold" in America. In 1540 Coronado left Mexico on a search for the golden cities. He crossed western Texas in 1541. Coronado saw Indian villages. But he didn't find cities of gold in Texas or anywhere else in America.

For many years the Spanish did little to settle Texas. Then in 1685 the Frenchman La Salle (lah SAL) built a colony on the Gulf Coast of southeast Texas. La Salle's colony was called Fort St. Louis (LOO • iss). Disease and an Indian raid ended this French outpost. But, seeing the French there, the Spanish felt that they must do something to take control of Texas.

Spanish priests, called *missionaries* (MISH • uh • nair • eez), were sent to Texas. Churches, called *missions*, were built. There the missionaries taught the Indians about Christianity. Forts were also built. There, Spanish soldiers guarded the missions.

In 1718 the Spanish built a mission and a fort at San Antonio (san an • TOH • nee • oh). In 1772 the little town of San Antonio became the center of the Spanish government in Texas. But by the late 1700s only a few thousand Spanish people had come to live in Texas.

In 1776 a new country was formed in America. It was the United States of America. Americans wanted to settle in Texas, which was still ruled by Spain. In 1820 Moses Austin (MOH • zez AW • stin) asked the Spanish government if he could bring American settlers to Texas. The answer was "Yes." Moses Austin died in 1821. His son, Stephen, then took over the work of settling Texas.

Stephen Austin brought thousands of Americans to Texas. They built log cabins. Many grew cotton. The Americans built towns. Washington-on-the-Brazos (BRAH • zos) and Columbus (coh • LUM • bus) were founded in 1821. In 1823 Stephen Austin founded San Felipe de Austin (san fay • LEEP day AW • stin). During the 1820s many Americans left notes saying "G.T.T." That meant that they had gone to Texas! Stephen Austin brought in so many settlers that he was called the "Father of Texas."

Stephen F. Austin (above) brought many
Americans to Texas (left).
One of the first areas of Texas
that Americans settled
was along the Brazos River (left).

In 1821—the same year that Stephen Austin began
Texas settlement—Mexico freed itself from Spain. Now
Mexico ruled Texas.

The Mexican government didn't want the Americans
to take control of Texas. In 1830 Mexico passed a law to
stop Americans from settling in Texas. Texans didn't like
this. They met at San Felipe de Austin in 1835. They
formed their own government. That year, Texans began
the war to free themselves from Mexican rule.

Texans took control of San Antonio on December 11, 1835. This greatly angered the Mexican General Santa Anna (san • tah ANN • ah). Santa Anna formed an army of 5,000 men. They marched towards San Antonio.

In San Antonio, the Americans went into an old mission called the Alamo. A number of famous American fighters were at the Alamo. Jim Bowie (BOO • ee) was there. He was known for fighting with a kind of knife called the bowie knife. The hunter and soldier Davy Crockett was also at the Alamo. But in all, the Americans had less than 200 men.

When Santa Anna arrived with his army he told the Americans to surrender. The Americans knew they couldn't beat 5,000 soldiers. But they chose to fight. "I shall never surrender or retreat . . . VICTORY OR DEATH," the American leader William Barret Travis wrote in a famous message.

The Alamo at night

Day after day the Mexican army pounded the Alamo with cannon fire. The Americans fired back. Then their ammunition ran low. On March 6, 1836, thousands of Mexican soldiers charged the Alamo. They climbed the walls and entered the building. The outnumbered Americans fought them until every American soldier at the Alamo was killed.

They didn't die in vain. As the battle raged, Texans met at Washington-on-the-Brazos. They wrote a declaration of independence. This said that Texas was free of Mexico. Texans also chose Sam Houston (HEW • stin) as leader of their army. By not giving up at the Alamo, the men there gave General Houston time to build his army.

In April of 1836 about 1,000 Americans under Sam Houston prepared to fight an army of about 1,400 under Santa Anna. "Victory is certain!" Houston told his men. "Trust in God and fear not! And remember the Alamo! Remember the Alamo!"

On April 21, 1836, Houston and his men attacked. In this fight—the Battle of San Jacinto (san jah • SIN • toh)—the Mexican army was beaten. Santa Anna was taken prisoner. Texas had freed itself from Mexico.

Texas was now a nation. It was called the Republic of Texas. Sam Houston was made president of the republic. The Republic of Texas even printed its own money.

Detail from the *Surrender of Santa Anna* by William Henry Huddle. It shows the captured Mexican general being brought before Sam Houston, who is lying under the tree.

But the Republic of Texas had big problems. The government didn't have enough money. And there was still a chance that Mexico would invade Texas. Sam Houston and most other Texans felt that Texas would be better off if it joined the United States.

On December 29, 1845, Texas became our 28th state. Austin was the state capital. The Texas flag has a single star on it. That is why Texas is nicknamed the *Lone Star State*.

During the 1850s, thousands of farmers came to Texas. Cotton was the big crop. Black slaves did the work on some large farms, called *plantations*.

In the 1850s, Americans in the North and the South argued about slavery. Southerners feared that the United States government would end slavery. Southerners spoke of States' Rights. This was the idea that each state should decide for itself about taxes, slavery, and other issues.

Finally, Southern states left the United States. They formed their own country—the Confederate (con • FED • er • it) States of America.

Texans had much in common with other Southerners. Many had come from Alabama, Mississippi, and other Southern states. Some Texans owned slaves. Texas left the United States and in March of 1861 it joined the South.

Texans recreate a Civil War battle.

War between the United States (North) and the Confederate States (South) began in April of 1861. This was the start of the Civil War. Texas sent over 50,000 soldiers to fight for the South. Texas also supplied the South with clothing, guns, and other materials.

But the South didn't have enough men or supplies to win the Civil War. By 1865 the South was beaten. That same year, on June 19, Texas slaves were freed. In 1870 Texas once again became part of the United States.

Texas longhorn

A good way to remember early Texas history is to think of the six flags that have flown there. They were the flags of Spain, France, Mexico, Republic of Texas, Confederate States of America, and the United States.

By the 1870s a new period in Texas history was under way. This was the period of the great "cattle drives."

Texas longhorn cattle were raised on the state's ranches. Cowboys on horseback drove the cattle herds north over the Chisholm (CHIZ • um) and Western trails. The cowboys took the cattle all the way to Kansas. From Kansas, the Texas cattle were sent north and east by train. They were made into beef.

Texas cowboys became famous. They wore big ten-gallon hats and high-heeled boots. The hats kept the sun out of their eyes. The boots gave them a good grip on the stirrups. Cowboys wore guns. Mostly they were fired to scare wild animals away from the cattle.

Just for fun, Texas cowboys told "tall tales." Some were about a cowboy named Pecos Bill. According to these stories, Bill could ride a mountain lion as well as a horse. He was only thrown when he tried to ride a tornado. Cowboys also said that it was Pecos Bill who dug the riverbed for the Rio Grande!

Modern cowboys roping cattle. At one time, cowboys on long cattle drives would make up songs and sing them to the cattle to keep them quiet at night.

The big cattle drives ended when railroads were built into Texas in the 1880s. Now cattle were sent directly east and north by train. The trains also brought in many settlers who set up small farms. By 1900, the population of Texas was 3,048,710. Most of the state's people worked at ranching and farming.

In 1901 a new treasure was found in Texas. This was oil. It gushed from the Spindletop oil field, near Beaumont (BOH • mont). Oil was called "black gold" because it was worth a lot of money. It was needed to run cars and machines. Later, oil was found in many places in Texas. Natural gas—used to cook food and heat buildings—was also found in the Lone Star State.

One of the earliest oil wells in Texas. The oil shot up for nine days until the well was capped.

Meat products like sausage (left), and
petroleum and natural gas products such
as butane (above), are important in Texas.

Manufacturing (making things in factories) also
became important in the 1900s. Oil refining became a
huge industry. The making of chemicals became
important. Meat packing and the making of other foods
became very big. More and more people left the farm
areas. They moved into cities to work in the factories.
Houston, Dallas (DAL • is), and San Antonio became
three of the biggest cities in the United States.

The astronauts on the Apollo 12 mission to the moon were guided from the Johnson Space Center near Houston.

Texas was the birthplace of two men who became president of the United States during the 1900s.

Dwight David Eisenhower (1890-1969) was born in Denison (DEN • ih • sun). "Ike" moved to Kansas when he was about two years old. From 1953 to 1961 he served as the 34th president of the United States.

Lyndon Baines Johnson (1908-1973) was born near Stonewall. He served as our 36th president.

While Lyndon Johnson was president, the space program became important. In 1964 a center for manned space flights began operating near Houston. At first it was called the Manned Spacecraft Center. Later its name was changed to the Lyndon B. Johnson Space Center.

Manufacturing (above) and producing oil (left) are two of the biggest Texas industries.

If Texans from the 1800s could visit the state today, they'd feel at home in many ways. They'd see that Texas is our leading cotton-growing and beef-raising state. But they'd also see that much has changed. Texas is now the leading state for producing oil. It's the second leading state for producing natural gas. The way people make a living has also greatly changed. Today, many more Texans work at manufacturing than at farming and ranching.

You have learned about some Texas history. Now it is time for a trip—in words and pictures—through the Lone Star State.

If you did a jigsaw puzzle of the United States, you could easily find the Texas piece. It would be the second biggest! Once you had your puzzle together you'd see that Mexico is to the south of Texas. The large body of water called the Gulf of Mexico is to the southeast. That part of Texas that sticks up like a chimney in the northwest is called the *Panhandle*.

Texas has almost every kind of scenery. Much of Texas is made of flat lands known as *plains*. Texas also has mountains—such as the Chisos (CHI • zohss) and Guadalupe (gwah • dah • LOOP) mountains. The Rio Grande, which separates Texas from Mexico, is just one of the state's many rivers. Along the Gulf of Mexico Texas also has sandy beaches and islands.

Texas has many kinds of scenery:
the flat valley of the Rio Grande
(top), the beaches of the Gulf Coast
(above left), stony deserts (above right),
and towering mountains (bottom) are
just some of them.

Left: Dallas Historical Plaza
Right: Reunion Tower

Dallas is in northeastern Texas. In 1841 a man named John Neely Bryan moved here from Arkansas. He built a hut and trading post on the Trinity (TRIN • ih • tee) River. The town of Dallas grew here as more settlers arrived.

If John Neely Bryan could visit Dallas today, you'd want to take him to the top of the 50-story Reunion Tower. From there he would see that "Big D" is now a huge city of banks, hotels, highways, and factories.

Many products are made in Dallas. Airplanes are made there. Clothes are a big Dallas product. Computers and soft drinks are made there. Dallas is also headquarters for many oil and insurance companies.

Left: Dallas City Hall
Above: A roller coaster at Six Flags Over Texas

You'll see many kinds of people as you walk through Dallas. You'll see many blacks. You'll see American Indians. You'll also meet people of Mexican, German, and many other ethnic backgrounds.

There are many interesting places to visit in Dallas. At the Dallas Museum of Natural History you can learn about the plants and animals of the Lone Star State. At the Dallas Museum of Fine Arts you can enjoy paintings and other famous artworks.

One place you're sure to like is Six Flags Over Texas, near Dallas. It's a big amusement park named for the six flags that flew over Texas.

Dallas is an important education center. Southern Methodist University, the University of Dallas, and the University of Texas at Dallas are just three of the schools in the area.

"Big D" is also a big sports center. The Dallas Cowboys play football in Texas Stadium, near Dallas. The Cowboys have won the Super Bowl twice—so far. Every New Year's Day a famous college football game is held in Dallas. It's called the Cotton Bowl. A major league baseball team, the Texas Rangers, plays not far from Dallas in Arlington (ARE • ling • ton).

Below: Texas Stadium
Right: A cattle auction in Fort Worth

The skyline of Fort Worth

Fort Worth is west of Dallas. Fort Worth was founded in 1849. At first it was an army post where soldiers protected settlers from Indian attacks. During the 1870s, Fort Worth was a stopping point for cowboys who were driving cattle north. Gamblers and gunslingers walked the streets of Fort Worth then.

Today, Fort Worth is one of our country's main cities for making aircraft. Airplanes are made there. So are helicopters. Food products and equipment for oil wells are also made here.

At the Log Cabin Village you can see the homes of some of Fort Worth's first settlers. The Amon Carter Museum of Western Art is also fun. Paintings by the Western artists Charles M. Russell and Frederic Remington can be viewed there.

Texas is a big state for education. South of Fort Worth you will come to the city of Waco (WAY • koh). Baylor University is there. Founded in 1845, Baylor is the oldest of Texas' many colleges.

From Waco, head to the capital of the Lone Star State, Austin. It was named for the "Father of Texas," Stephen Austin. Austin has been the permanent capital of Texas since 1845, the year Texas became a state.

Visit the State Capitol building. Lawmakers from all across the state meet in this pink granite building. You can watch them as they work on laws for Texas.

Above left: The Austin skyline
Right: The Lyndon Baines Johnson Library
and Museum
Below left: The State Capitol building

Many of Austin's people work for the government. Others work at nearby Bergstrom (BERG • strum) Air Force Base.

Have you noticed all the students in Austin? The University of Texas has its largest campus there. About 45,000 students attend this school.

The Lyndon Baines Johnson Library and Museum is in Austin. There you can learn about President Johnson and the office of the presidency. You'll also enjoy the Texas Memorial Museum. There you can learn about the history of the Lone Star State.

Mission San Jose
is a very old
Spanish-built church.

San Antonio is southwest of Austin. San Antonio began in 1718, when the Spanish built a mission and fort here. The Spanish built a number of missions in San Antonio. Visit Mission San Jose (san HOH • zay), which was built in 1720. It is nicknamed the "Queen of Missions" because it is so beautiful.

Visit another San Antonio mission, the Alamo. The Alamo is called the "Cradle of Texas Liberty."

About half of the people in San Antonio are of Mexican or Spanish background. La Villita (lah vee • EE • tah), meaning "Little Village" in Spanish, shows what a Spanish Texas town of the 1800s looked like.

The new and the old in San Antonio:
Riverwalk (above) and La Villita (left)

Although San Antonio is a very historic city, the
people who live there now must make a living. Many
work at Fort Sam Houston and the other nearby military
bases. Clothes and food products are also made here.

From San Antonio, head to Houston in southeastern
Texas. Once, Karankawa Indians lived here. The city
was founded in 1836 by Augustus and John Allen, who
were brothers. They named the city after Sam Houston.
Today, Houston is the biggest city in Texas. It is also the
fastest-growing major city in our country.

An oil refinery, where crude oil is made into many products

There is a wealth of oil in the Houston area. Oil is made into gasoline and other products at refineries. The Houston region is our country's leading center for refining oil.

A lot of chemicals are made in Houston. Rubber, paper, and foods are also made here. Houston products leave the city by train, plane, and truck. Boats take Houston products to many cities of the world. The boats go through the Houston Ship Channel to the Gulf of Mexico.

Visit the Houston Museum of Fine Arts. There you can see world-famous art. At the Jesse H. Jones Hall for Performing Arts you can hear symphony concerts and watch operas and ballet.

Downtown Houston. Houston is one of the fastest-growing cities in the United States.

Go to the Lyndon B. Johnson Space Center near Houston. You will see a spacecraft that went to the moon and back. And you will see how scientists there guide ships that are 250,000 miles out in space.

Unless you've been living on the moon, you've heard of the Houston Astrodome! It's a big indoor sports stadium. The Houston Astros play baseball in the Astrodome. The pro football Houston Oilers also play there.

From Houston, head south to the Gulf of Mexico. The Gulf of Mexico splashes against more than 360 miles of Texas shore. The land along the water is called the *Gulf Coast.*

Texas' Gulf Coast is a big vacation area. People sunbathe on its beaches. They boat and swim in the Gulf of Mexico. Lots of people come here in the winter. While it's freezing in northern cities in January, it is often 70° along the Gulf Coast.

The Gulf Coast is sometimes struck by hurricanes. Hurricanes are big storms that form over the ocean. They smash land with winds of over 100 miles per hour. They cause giant waves and floods. In 1900 a hurricane hit the city of Galveston (GAL • vess • tun), on Galveston Island. About 6,000 people were killed. This was one of the worst disasters in United States history.

Galveston is now protected by a big seawall. In times of hurricanes, this wall keeps Galveston from flooding.

Left: The seawall at Galveston helps protect the city
from flooding during hurricanes.
Above: Galveston Island

Stories are told of pirate treasure buried on islands off
the Gulf Coast. At one time the pirate Jean Laffite
(JAHN la • FEET) lived on Galveston Island. Today, you
won't see pirate ships sailing near the coast. You will see
fishing boats, though. Texas fishermen bring back
shrimps, crabs, oysters, and red snapper. Texas is one of
our leading shrimp-producing states.

Above: View of Corpus Christi
Riding horses on one of Corpus Christi's beaches

Corpus Christi (KOR • pus KRISS • tee), on the Gulf
Coast, is an important seaport. Chemicals and oil
products made there go by boat to other cities of the
world.

From Corpus Christi, take a trip into far southern
Texas. You'll see towns with Spanish names in this area.
San Juan, Zapata (zah • PAH • tah), San Benito (san ben •
EE • toh), and Rio Hondo (REE • oh HON • doh) are just
four of them. You'll meet many Mexican-Americans
here. Over 20 percent of all Texans are of Mexican or
Spanish background.

Head into western Texas. It doesn't have as many big cities as eastern Texas. But it does have lots of oil wells, farms, and ranches. The oil wells remind you that Texas is the leading oil-producing state. Texas also has the most farms of any state.

Many crops are grown in western Texas—and in other parts of the state. Grain sorghum is one of the main crops. It is used to feed livestock. Rice, sugar cane, wheat, spinach, and peanuts are some other Texas crops. The Lone Star State is the leader for growing cotton.

Harvesting rice

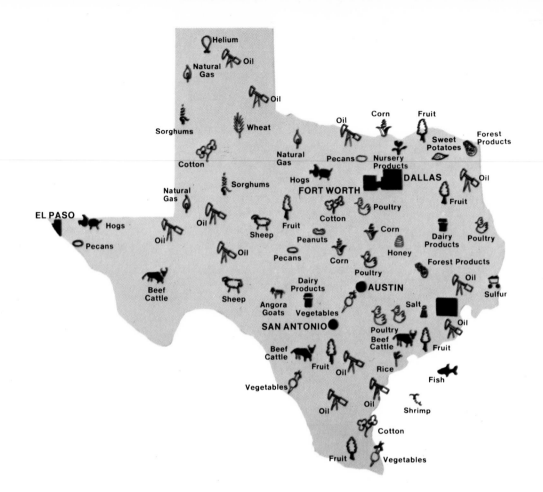

Western Texas is also a big area for raising beef cattle. In all, there are about 15 million beef cattle in Texas. That means that the state has more cattle than people. Many of the cattle are sent to Amarillo (am • ah • RILL • oh), in northwest Texas. The cattle are sold there. They are then made into beef.

Texas is the leading state for raising sheep as well as cattle. Hogs, chickens, and riding horses are also raised by Texas farmers and ranchers.

Finish your trip by going to El Paso (el PASS • oh), in far western Texas. The city lies on the Rio Grande, just across from Mexico. Cattle are raised and cotton is grown near El Paso. A lot of cotton clothes are made in the city.

The oldest community in what is now Texas can be seen in El Paso. It is called Ysleta (ee • SLET • ah). It was built by Spanish missionaries and Tigua (TEE • gwa) Indians in 1682. Tigua Indians still live there.

Places can't tell the whole story of Texas. Many interesting people have lived in the Lone Star State.

Samuel Houston (1793-1863) was born in Virginia. At 15, he ran away from home. He lived with the Cherokee (CHAIR • uh • kee) Indians for three years. Later, Houston became a lawyer, a soldier, and a Tennessee lawmaker. In the 1830s, Sam Houston moved to Texas. Houston led the army in the fight to free Texas from Mexico. He was president of the Republic of Texas. He

Sam Houston

served as United States senator, and then as governor of the state. During the Civil War, Governor Houston did not want Texas to join the South. But he was put out of office and died in Huntsville during the war.

Quanah (KWAH • nah) was born near Lubbock (LUB • uck). Quanah became chief of the Comanche (koh • MAN • chee) Indians. Quanah saw hunters wiping out the buffalo. He saw his people being pushed off their lands. During the 1860s and 1870s, Quanah, a fierce man in battle, led raids on settlements. But in 1874, he was beaten in a fight at Adobe Walls, in Texas. Quanah then had to live on an Oklahoma reservation. There he founded schools for his people. He taught them to make money by renting lands to cattlemen. The town of Quanah, Texas, was named for him.

Miriam A. Ferguson (1875-1961) was born in Bell County. Her husband—James E. Ferguson—was a Texas governor. Later, she also became governor of the Lone Star State. "Ma" Ferguson was one of the first woman governors of a state.

Lyndon Baines Johnson (1908-1973) was born in a farmhouse near Stonewall. He grew up in Johnson City. As a young man, Lyndon hitchhiked up and down the West Coast. He made money by washing dishes and waiting on tables. When he returned home, Johnson told his parents, "I'm sick of working just with my hands." He said he was ready to work with his brain. Lyndon Johnson became a teacher. Later he was elected

Left: Lyndon Baines Johnson
Right: Barbara Jordan

congressman and then United States senator from Texas.
Then, in 1960, Lyndon Johnson was elected vice-president of the United States. When President John F. Kennedy was killed in 1963, Johnson became president. The next year, in 1964, "LBJ" ran for president on his own. He won.

Barbara Jordan was born in Houston in 1936. When she was very young, she decided that she would become something special. Barbara Jordan became a lawyer. Later, she ran for public office. She was the first black woman to become a state senator in Texas. In 1972

Texans elected her to the United States House of Representatives. She became the first Southern black woman to serve in the House.

Alan Bean was born in Wheeler, in 1932. He became an astronaut. In November of 1969 he spent over a full day on the moon.

Texas has also produced many famous sports stars. Rogers Hornsby (1896-1963) was born in Winters. In 1924 Hornsby hit for an amazing .424 average. That's the highest batting average in modern baseball. The great baseball players Ernie Banks and Frank Robinson were also born in Texas.

Jack Johnson (1878-1946) was born in Galveston. He was the heavyweight boxing champion of the world from 1908 to 1915. He was the first black to win the heavyweight title.

A.J. Foyt, born in Houston in 1935, has won the "Indianapolis 500" race four times.

Sunset over the Texas Panhandle

Once home to Indians and Spanish missionaries.

Now home to ranchers . . . farmers . . . and oil workers.

The state where you can see the Alamo . . . the Johnson Space Center . . . and the Houston Astrodome.

The leading state for raising cattle . . . producing oil . . . and growing cotton.

This is Texas—the Lone Star State!

Facts About TEXAS

Area—267,338 square miles (our 2nd biggest state, after Alaska)

Greatest Distance North to South—801 miles

Greatest Distance East to West—773 miles

Borders—New Mexico, Oklahoma, and Arkansas to the north; Oklahoma, Arkansas, and Louisiana to the east; Mexico and the Gulf of Mexico to the south; Mexico and New Mexico to the west

Highest Point—8,751 feet above sea level (Guadalupe Peak)

Lowest Point—Sea level, along the coast of the Gulf of Mexico

Hottest Recorded Temperature—120° (at Seymour, on August 12, 1936)

Coldest Recorded Temperature—Minus 23° (at Tulia, on February 12, 1899, and also at Seminole, on February 8, 1933)

Statehood—Our 28th state, on December 29, 1845

Origin of Name—*Texas* comes from the Caddo Indian word *Tejas,* meaning *friends*

Capital—Austin (since 1845)

Counties—254

U.S. Senators—2

U.S. Representatives—27

State Senators—31

State Representatives—150

State Song—"Texas, Our Texas," by Gladys Yoakum Wright and William J. Marsh

State Motto—*Friendship*

Nickname—*The Lone Star State*

State Flag—Adopted in 1839

State Seal—Adopted in 1846

State Flower—Bluebonnet

State Bird—Mockingbird

State Tree—Pecan

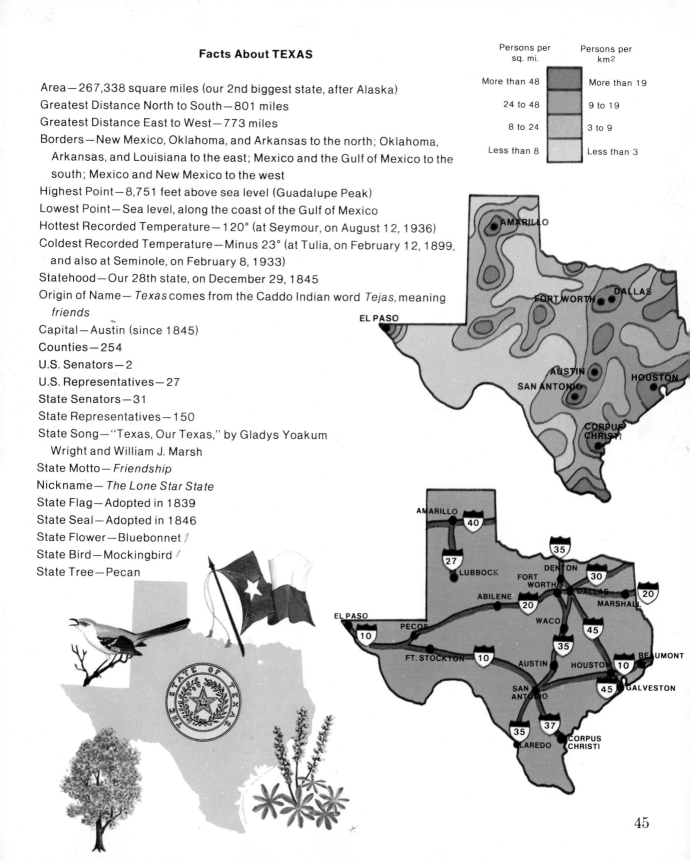

Persons per sq. mi.		Persons per km2
More than 48		More than 19
24 to 48		9 to 19
8 to 24		3 to 9
Less than 8		Less than 3

Some Rivers—Rio Grande, Pecos, Red, Brazos, Canadian, Sabine, Neches, Trinity, Colorado, Guadalupe

Main Mountain Ranges—Guadalupe, Chisos, Davis

Some Islands—Galveston, Padre, Matagorda, St.Joseph, Mustang

Wildlife—Deer, pronghorn antelope, javelinas, squirrels, coyotes, bobcats, mountain lions, foxes, rattlesnakes and other snakes, alligators, wild turkeys, quail, roadrunners, woodpeckers, mockingbirds, pelicans, many other kinds of birds

Fishing—Shrimps, oysters, crabs, red snapper, trout

Farm Products—Beef cattle, grain sorghum, cotton, rice, wheat, sugar cane, sugar beets, peanuts, pecans, soybeans, corn, oats, hay, cabbage, spinach, watermelons, chickens, eggs, milk, turkeys, sheep, hogs, riding horses, honey, oranges, grapefruit, peaches, strawberries

Mining—Oil, natural gas, sulfur, salt

Manufacturing—Chemicals, petroleum and coal products, machinery, packaged foods, airplanes and other transportation equipment, clothes, paper products

Population—1980 census: 16,228,383 (1985 estimate: 16,370,000)

Major Cities	1980 Census	1984 Estimate
Houston	1,595,138	1,705,700
Dallas	904,599	974,200
San Antonio	785,927	842,800
El Paso	425,259	463,800
Fort Worth	385,164	414,600
Austin	345,890	397,000
Corpus Christi	232,138	285,100

Texas History

There were people in Texas over 11,000 years ago

1519—Alonso Alvarez de Piñeda explores and maps the Texas coast for Spain

1528—The Spaniard Cabeza De Vaca is shipwrecked on the Texas coast

1541—While searching for gold, Coronado passes through Texas

1682—The Spanish build the first two missions in Texas, near what is now El Paso

1685—The Frenchman La Salle founds Fort Saint Louis on Texas' Gulf Coast; disease and an Indian attack soon end this colony

1690—The Spanish build their first mission in east Texas, near what is now Weches

1718—Spanish build a mission and a fort at San Antonio

1744—Besides Indians, only about 1,500 people live in Texas

1749—The town of Goliad is founded

1772—San Antonio becomes the center for Spanish government in Texas

1779—The town of Nacogdoches is founded

1813—*Gaceta de Texas*, the first newspaper, is printed in Nacogdoches

1830—Mexico passes a law to stop Americans from going to Texas

1835—Fight to free Texas from Mexico begins

1836—Big year in Texas history! March 2: Texans issue a declaration of independence saying they are free of Mexico. March 6: The Mexican army kills all the defenders of the Alamo. April 21: Sam Houston beats the Mexican army under Santa Anna at the Battle of San Jacinto. September 1: Sam Houston is elected president of the independent Republic of Texas

1845—On December 29, Texas becomes our 28th state; Austin is the capital

1861-1865—During the Civil War, over 50,000 Texans fight on the side of the Confederacy

1863—While the Civil War rages, Sam Houston dies at Huntsville on July 26

1865—The last battle of the Civil War is fought at Palmito Hill in Texas on May 13; on June 19 Texas slaves are declared free

1870—Texas once again is part of the United States

1870s—Big cattle drives from Texas to Kansas are under way; this period lasts until railroads cross Texas in the 1880s

1883—University of Texas opens at Austin

1888—State Capitol building is completed at Austin

1890—Dwight David Eisenhower is born at Denison, Texas

1900—A hurricane kills 6,000 at Galveston

1901—Discovery of Spindletop oil field begins oil boom

1908—Lyndon Baines Johnson is born near Stonewall, Texas

1917-1918—Over 200,000 Texans serve in World War I

1920—Population of the Lone Star State is 4,663,228

1924—Mrs. Miriam A. Ferguson is elected governor of Texas; she is the second woman governor in our country

1941-1945—750,000 Texans serve in World War II; Audie Murphy, born in Kingston, earns the most medals of any U.S. soldier

1945—Happy 100th birthday, Lone Star State!

1950—Texas population reaches, 7,711,194

1952—Dwight D. Eisenhower is elected 34th president of the United States

1953—Tornadoes kill 146 in Texas

1963—When President John F. Kennedy is shot to death in Dallas on November 22, Lyndon Baines Johnson becomes our 36th president

1964—Lyndon B. Johnson is elected president; the Manned Spacecraft Center near Houston becomes the headquarters for manned flights

1972—Barbara Jordan, born in Houston, becomes the first Southern black woman elected to the U.S. House of Representatives

1973—President Johnson dies in San Antonio; the Manned Spacecraft Center is renamed the Lyndon B. Johnson Space Center

1977—The National Women's Conference is held in Houston

1986—Falling oil prices result in 10.5 percent unemployment, highest since Great Depression; Mark White re-elected governor

INDEX

About the Author:
   Dennis Fradin attended Northwestern University on a creative writing scholarship and was graduated in 1967. While still at Northwestern, he published his first stories. A prolific writer, Dennis Fradin has been regularly publishing stories in such diverse places as *The Saturday Evening Post*, *Scholastic*, *National Humane Review*, *Midwest*, and *The Teaching Paper*. He has also scripted several educational films. Since 1970 he has taught second grade reading in a Chicago school—a rewarding job, which, the author says, "provides a captive audience on whom I test my children's stories." Married and the father of three children, Dennis Fradin spends his free time with his family.

About the Artist:
   Len Meents studied painting and drawing at Southern Illinois University and after graduation in 1969 he moved to Chicago. Mr. Meents works full time as a painter and illustrator. He and his wife and child currently make their home in LaGrange, Illinois.